PAMPHLETS ON AMERICAN WRITERS · NUMBER 67

UNIVERSITY OF MINNESOTA

⌁ *Edmund Wilson*

BY WARNER BERTHOFF

UNIVERSITY OF MINNESOTA PRESS · MINNEAPOLIS

Printed in the United States of America at
the North Central Publishing Co., St. Paul

Library of Congress Catalog Card Number: 68-64750

PUBLISHED IN GREAT BRITAIN, INDIA, AND PAKISTAN BY THE OXFORD
UNIVERSITY PRESS, LONDON, BOMBAY, AND KARACHI, AND IN CANADA
BY THE COPP CLARK PUBLISHING CO. LIMITED, TORONTO

EDMUND WILSON

↗ *Edmund Wilson*

THE American literary critic and journalist Edmund Wilson was born May 8, 1895, at Red Bank in the Atlantic Highlands–Asbury Park angle of the New Jersey coast, a district originally composed of independent towns and villages but during his early life being steadily absorbed into the suburban, summer-resort sprawl of metropolitan New York. The transformation seems prophetic; it presents in miniature the pattern of all those developments and changes in society at large which have produced the distrustful outlook on modern progress that Wilson has held to most of his life. One may feel that this outlook was his chief inheritance. His father, for whom he was named, was a lawyer and civil servant of distinction who became attorney general of New Jersey under both Republican and Democratic administrations but refused various federal appointments: a moody, self-absorbed man, as Wilson describes him, tending to be impatient and peremptory with others and subject in his later life to "neurotic eclipses" requiring periodic withdrawals and retreats. The family background was upper middle class, college oriented, and professional — lawyers, doctors, ministers, and, later, board members and museum managers — with a sprinkling of more exotic figures: the Virginia cousins whom Wilson subsequently identified with the charming, aimless aristocrats of *The Cherry Orchard*; an aunt who married a French painter descended from the Egyptologist Champollion and killed on the Western Front in 1915.

Two autobiographical sketches, "The Author at Sixty" in *A Piece of My Mind* (1956) and "Family" in the recently published volume of early journals, *A Prelude* (1967), delineate very precisely the qualities of this life and background — the tangle of family relationships, intense, self-nourishing, untranslatable to outsiders; the cultural snobbery; the insulation and stuffiness of a clan easily scandalized yet tolerant and protective with its own delinquents, being finally indifferent to general opinion; the combination of outward assurance and parlor hysterics and melancholia; the erratic blend of sexual and imaginative repression and leisure-class self-indulgence; the custom of marrying within a limited circle of social familiars but on perhaps no other basis of compatibility, "because there was no one else"; and, at the root, the loss of contact in an investment-trust era with the traditional functions of a property-owning gentry. For people of this class, privilege was no defense against instability and disorientation. "Of my father's close friends at college," Wilson has written, "but a single one was left by the time he was in his thirties: all the rest were dead — some had committed suicide."

After a family tour of Europe in 1908 Wilson entered the Hill School in Pottstown, where he endured a cramping regime devoted to evangelical uplift and the avoidance of unclean thoughts but where he also received sound training in Greek and Latin. In 1912 he went on to Princeton, concentrating there on modern literature and language and writing essays, poems, stories, and parodies for the *Nassau Lit*. At each school he found a teacher of superior character and gifts — Alfred Rolfe at the Hill, Christian Gauss at Princeton — whose influence upon him he would later handsomely acknowledge. Wilson's memoirs of these humanely principled men are in fact outstanding among his portrait-essays, having that core motive of personal attachment and identification that regularly distinguishes his best work as a critical observer. At Princeton, too, he fell in with an exceptionally gifted and ambitious company of undergraduate writers. T. K. Whipple, John Bishop, and Scott Fitzgerald were close friends and collaborators on the *Lit*; for each of them too Edmund Wilson would eventually serve as memoirist and literary executor.

After Princeton he worked as a cub on the *New York Evening Sun* and then, in the summer of 1917, enlisted in a hospital unit and was in France for a year and a half. "My experience of the army," he writes in *A Prelude*, "had had on me a liberating effect. I could now get on with all kinds of people and could satisfy my curiosity about aspects of life that otherwise I should not perhaps so soon have known." It was a disillusioning and angering experience as well, with an impact much like that recorded in the war books of Wilson's American contemporaries, Dos Passos, Hemingway, E. E. Cummings, Thomas Boyd. Besides a few deromanticizing stories of his own — one, "The Death of a Soldier," appeared in *The Undertaker's Garland*, a miscellany of apprentice work in prose and verse published with John Peale Bishop in 1922 — Wilson's literary response to the war took the form of a manifesto, composed at an occupation GHQ in Germany, which "indicted the institutions of the Western world and suggested a way out in the direction of socialism." At the same time (as he later wrote in *The American Jitters*, in 1932) he had decided that he "could never go back to the falseness and dullness of my prewar life again. I swore to myself that when the War was over I should stand outside society altogether." It was not the last time he would sound a secessionist note.

In the early 1920's, confident that the arts were thriving despite all the restlessness and disorder of postwar society, Wilson committed himself to a career in literature and settled down to writing essays, reviews, and sketches for various New York papers: among others *Vanity Fair*, of which he was managing editor during 1920–21, the *Liberator* and the *Dial*, and finally the *New Republic*, which he joined as an associate editor in 1926. His writings of this period, including plays and fictional sketches, are brimful of literary attitudes and circumstances characteristic of the American twenties. Continually, despite his resolve to "stand outside society" and devote himself to the great transcendent human interests, he returns to that preoccupation with the issue of American cultural maturity which Van Wyck Brooks in particular, in studies like *America's Coming-of-Age*, had defined for this era. At the same time, in discussing new work, Wilson showed himself an alert and precisely sympathetic advocate of the creative revolution of his time; he was far freer in greeting all its remarkable innovations and triumphs than Brooks, only nine years his senior, ever learned to be. Wilson's first important book, the novel *I Thought of Daisy* (1929), joins these two period concerns. The form of his novel he thought of as experimental, in the art-fashion of the day – he later described it as "a sort of symphonic arrangement . . . like *Ulysses* and *À la Recherche du Temps Perdu*" – while the theme is the effort of the narrator, an American intellectual whose literary friends represent various characteristic attitudes and philosophies of the era, to make invigorating connections with common American life (represented by Daisy) and so close the disabling gap between common reality and abstract literary ideas about it, between "the self that experiences and the self that writes."

I Thought of Daisy resolves this theme satisfactorily in the moving peroration that closes the last chapter, with its vision of a universal acceptance of the reality created and shared by all who are alive together in one place and time. But Wilson himself, three years later at the end of his Depression chronicle, *The American Jitters*, was very much less sanguine about the twenties milieu he had commemorated in his novel: "I always felt so little at home in the American prosperity era, though I made earnest efforts to enjoy it and to believe that it was beneficial to other people (not exercising enough insight to know that it was bound for the rocks), that I am not sorry to see it all go glimmering." He closed

8

this testament with an affirmative credo, but what is affirmed is as materialistic in its premises, and as vague, as the reassurances of any Chamber of Commerce publicist: a belief in "progress" (symbolized by the convenience-enhancing achievements of modern technology) and, more generally, in "human evolution," leading to the bracing thought that "we" as "beings" are sure to develop "into something higher still." It was an anachronistic, "eighteenth-century" belief, Wilson confessed, and it merged rather wishfully into a vision of some purified future of renewed human nobility. Seemingly, Wilson's voiced confidence in the vocation of letters and its uses, though primed by the heady victories of contemporary art, could now find broader social confirmation only in carefully nourished visionary states: in a simplified picture of certain epochs in the past which had produced great literature, and in the regenerate historical future promised by ideological Marxism — to the study of which, as the crisis of the Depression deepened, he had begun to direct his attention.

At no point in his long career does Edmund Wilson strike us as profound or original in his presentation of systems of thought and imagination, yet this persistent element of serious, thoroughgoing, personal concern gives his reports a vividness and an urgency that fix them in the mind. From his earliest reviews he had known how to make his subjects interesting — the *sine qua non* of effective journalism. In the late twenties, alongside an undiminished output of shorter pieces, he had begun to write more extended critical studies characterized by a richer blend of historical consideration, a fuller review of each author's career, and a more sustained effort of consecutive description. These studies, brought together under some attention-focusing title, became the books that in the next ten years gained Wilson a place of his own in his time's literature.

In *Axel's Castle* (1931) a whole new American generation of students learned about Symbolism and its central role in modern writing, and discovered for perhaps the first time something of the artistic logic behind the work of authors like Valéry, Joyce, and Proust. In *The Triple Thinkers* (1938) Wilson helped to keep current the Flaubertian doctrine of the disinterestedness and sacrificial heroism of the true artist. In the essays composing *The Wound and the Bow* (1941) he used, with intelligence and discrimination, Freudian insights as well as a consciousness of the political malaise of the thirties to show off both the inward complexity in the writings of several mostly out-of-fashion authors — the essays on Dickens and Kipling are outstanding in this respect — and also the relevance of their work to fundamental situations in common life; he emphasized, too, the personal courage, despite afflictions, with which these authors had persisted in their careers.

A steady widening of horizons and perspectives shows in other ways at this time and principally, as the thirties advanced, in his study of Marxism. In the disorder and confusion of literary thought during this decade — its political side is well described in Daniel Aaron's *Writers on the Left* — Wilson's personal course seems of a singular steadiness and integrity. A concern for social justice rises strongly to the surface. He traveled widely through the country filing on-the-scene reports of the suffering and violence of the Depression years, the labor struggles, relief offices, congressional hearings, the varied scenes of a nationwide demoralization. Sympathetic toward the Soviet Russian experiment, he was sharply critical of the hostility it aroused among Western liberals, a hostility, he felt, based on ignorance — or worse. There was an abrasive virtue in his recognition ("An Appeal to Progressives," 1931) that not only business leaders and politicians but liberal and progressive intellectuals — including the most honored recent spokesmen of the American public conscience, men like John Dewey, Charles Beard, Walter Lippmann, Justice Holmes — had all been "betting on capitalism" and were all implicated in the world crisis following on its huge civil failures in World War I and the Depression.

Wilson did not, however, become a Communist himself. Some unshakable critical fidelity to the fitness of word and occasion, and behind it that independence of judgment which has always, so to speak, made his yea, yea and his nay, nay, kept him from serving time as either party member or fellow traveler. (So, later, he was spared the necessity of apostasy and recantation over the Moscow trials and the Nazi-Soviet pact.) What he did instead was characteristic. He went to Russia to study and to look around for himself (it was his first trip abroad since 1919, for Wilson was one of the few important new writers of the twenties who had not joined in person the expatriate scramble to Paris); and he undertook a prolonged examination of the basic literature of revolutionary socialism, in particular the writings and memoirs of Marx, Engels, Lassalle, Bakunin, Trotsky, and Lenin. Out of this he produced, at the end of the decade, his ambitious "Study in the Writing and Acting of History," *To the Finland Station* (1940).

From this point forward there is a certain miscellaneousness about the profusion of Edmund Wilson's writing. He continued, as before, turning out occasional plays and stories that document the literary life of the period he himself had lived through; and with the story collection *Memoirs of Hecate County* (1946), one of the better books of American fiction in the lean forties, he had an unlooked-for *succès de scandale* by way of the sexual explicitness in his portraits of modern "damned souls." He was staff book reviewer for the *New Yorker* from 1944 to 1948 and continued after 1948 to publish literary articles there, also travel essays and personal memoirs. His caustic, disillusioned postwar report from "the ruins of Italy, Greece, and England,"

Europe without Baedeker (1947), was carried by the *New Yorker* as foreign correspondence, and later books like *The Scrolls from the Dead Sea* (1955), *Apologies to the Iroquois* (1960), *O Canada* (1965), and *A Prelude: Landscapes, Characters and Conversations from the Earlier Years of My Life* (1967) also appeared first in the *New Yorker*. (An exception was *The Cold War and the Income Tax* of 1963, the latest of his pamphlets dissociating himself from contemporary society.)

The manner of Wilson's casual book reviewing in the forties and fifties was, if anything, more assured than ever. It remained one of the pleasures of his critical style that he had nothing at all of the pontifical solemnness then flourishing in the Eliot-infected literary quarterlies. Yet if any American reviewer seemed to speak *ex cathedra*, it was he. The price of this authority, however, was for the first time a certain remoteness from current developments. He continued to write on new books and authors as well as established names. But his work was less and less an inclusive record of the literary temper and achievement of the present moment. (The new era, it must be said, was a less distinguished one than the twenties and much less in need of critical translation.) By his seventh decade — introduced with the crusty miscellany *A Piece of My Mind: Reflections at Sixty* (1956) — Wilson had become not so much a critic among other critics, other working contemporaries, as a public institution: an honorable but always rather saddening American fate.

There was no softening, however, of personal attitudes and no appearance of compromise or accommodation with the ethos of what he plainly felt to be a bad time, a deteriorating social order. In this most recent phase we still find Edmund Wilson, as in 1919 and 1932, affirming his disaffection from modern society as he regularly encounters it and as he understands its historical formation. He has done this in so many words and also, increasingly, through choice of subject. His last large-scale undertaking, *Patriotic Gore: Studies in the Literature of the American Civil War* (1962), is an examination of that time in earlier history when the American nation came closest to dissolution and of the effects of this ordeal on battle-shocked survivors; one may feel that nothing has yet been written of greater relevance to the civil-rights ordeal of the 1960's, and hardly anything that is more despairing in its implications. (The book's introduction, which bluntly compares the actions of national societies, democratic or otherwise, to the unreasoning behavior of sea slugs and insects, establishes a mood that suffuses all that follows.)

Even when he writes on subjects far removed from contemporary preoccupations, a relevance is suggested. The historical and textual origins of Christianity, the distinctive quality of Hebrew and Russian as instruments of expression, the morally suggestive findings of entomologists and mycologists, the struggles of fringe cultures (the New York State Iroquois) and minority languages (Hungarian) to survive in the modern mass-world — all furnish perspectives on the confusions of the present moment. Wilson even makes a show of out-and-out pedantry, though in a constructive vein. He studies dictionaries and grammars and laments their declining usefulness; he compiles lists of fashionable clichés, "words of ill omen," particularly the murderous euphemisms of the Cold War dialect and the huckster-jargon of slick literary and political journalism; he offers intelligent proposals for the teaching of classical literature and language, to stem the decline of old-fashioned humanistic education.

We also still find him, though less systematically than before, rummaging about on the open shelves of contemporary letters — reading Kingsley Amis, Lawrence Durrell, Edward Gorey, the later Angus Wilson, W. H. Auden in his American phase, Mario Praz, Stephen Potter, Robert Lowell, John Berryman — and as usual pointing out virtues that others might have noticed but had not brought into general consciousness or defining careers where nothing so prestige-laden had yet been seen to exist. Among active critics and journalists Wilson retains an unsurpassed ability not only to make one want to read the books he discusses but to compose believable pictures of continuing literary history. Past seventy, he remains what he has always been, a critical touchstone by which other readers and writers may better understand their own attitudes and findings, their own progressive experience of literature.

This practical devotion to the existing community of authors and readers and to the common mental life of his age has been the great sustaining virtue of Edmund Wilson's performance as a critic. It has not fallen to him to redirect fundamental literary history or to bring about momentous changes in taste and understanding — a fact that overenthusiastic assessments of his work (comparisons, for example, of *Axel's Castle* to Eliot's *The Sacred Wood*) fail to take into account. He has not been a lawgiver or theorist (his essay "The Historical Interpretation of Literature," 1940, is hardly more than a confession of personal interests); no critical school, no new lines of creative achievement, have developed from his work; nor have his books noticeably affected understanding of the essential nature of literary expressiveness and the "meaning of meaning," as did (to cite volumes of criticism published at the same moment as *Axel's Castle* but based on more sophisticated theoretical interests) William Empson's *Seven Types of Ambiguity* and Kenneth Burke's *Counter-Statement*. His own frequent assessments of his role and function have always been attractively modest. Where Eliot would write essays defining the universal "function of criticism" or the qualities of "the perfect critic," Wilson typically issued a set of practical instructions for authors and editors which he called, with multiple irony, "The

Literary Worker's Polonius" (1935). Short of positive insult, a flatter term than "literary worker" would be hard to find. In an earlier piece on "The Critic Who Does Not Exist" (1928) he was principally concerned with the simple lack of communication among authors and literary groups in the United States and with the failure of creative ideas to circulate productively. It is as a bringer of news, preferably good news, that he has seen himself; as a journalist in the most honorable sense; as a contributor to "the general cross-fertilization" ("A Modest Self-Tribute," 1952).

He has been quite explicit about this. Writing once of his disappointment when, full of the last installment of Proust's great novel and a swelling sense of the grandeur of the whole, he found that Thornton Wilder knew as much about it as he did, and knew it also at first hand, Wilson confessed: "There are few things I enjoy so much as talking to people about books which I have read but they haven't, and making them wish they had — preferably a book that is hard to get or in a language that they do not know" ("A Weekend at Ellerslie," 1952). In the 1948 Foreword to *The Triple Thinkers*, defending himself against the complaint that he sometimes had little to say about his subjects' most prominent or most characteristic qualities, he wrote, "my purpose has always been to try to contribute something new: I have aimed either to present some writer who was not well enough known or, in the case of a familiar writer, to call attention to some neglected aspect of his work or his career." Perhaps "Boswell" would be closer to the mark than "Polonius," if we can imagine a Boswell for an entire era, taking "literature as a whole" (as he wrote in the 1938 essay "Is Verse a Dying Technique?") for his field.

What Wilson has meant by "journalism" is nothing degrading or commonplace. From the start he chose impressive masters to guide his ambition, writers who in various ways had found scope in their journeywork for serious individual reflection and judgment. "We had grown up," he wrote of the situation of the twenties, "on the journalism of Shaw and Chesterton, Belloc and Max Beerbohm, and later, in the United States, of the Mencken and Nathan of the *Smart Set* and the Woollcott and Broun of the *World*. All these writers were everlastingly saying 'I': the exploitation of personality had become an integral part of criticism" (Foreword, *The Shores of Light*). And in ways that unfailingly give dramatic movement and suspense to his best longer essays, Wilson uses this first-person method himself. Returning to a familiar name or taking up some widely discussed new topic, he tells us what he has heard and been led to expect, and then how his expectation has been satisfied, disappointed, surprised, or overturned.

But the list of his early admirations gives only a part of his picture of himself as "literary worker" — unless Shaw's name in particular reminds us that an easy practical mastery of the subjects treated, and the hard work required to gain this mastery, are to be included by definition. "Reviewer critic" was another name for Wilson's conception of his role — an "extremely rare" being, he noted in the "Polonius" article — and the description offered there may be taken as an accurate summary of his own working program: "Such a reviewer should be more or less familiar, or be ready to familiarize himself, with the past work of every important writer he deals with and be able to write about an author's new book in the light of his general development and intention. He should also be able to see the author in relation to the national literature as a whole and the national literature in relation to other literatures. But this means a great deal of work, and it presupposes a certain amount of training." The article goes on to describe the minimum responsibility that goes with each new critical task: "The reviewer, at the very least, should be

16

expected to supply information. The retelling of the story of a novel, the summary of an historical or philosophical book, the selection of representative passages and the attempt to communicate the quality of a poet, is the most boring part of the reviewer's business, but it is an absolutely essential part. The reader should be given a chance to judge whether or not he would be interested in the book, irrespective of what the reviewer may think of it; and it is an indispensable discipline for the reviewer, or any critic, to give the gist of the book in his own words. . . . It is as vitally important for the critic to establish definite identities for the books that he discusses in an essay as it is for the novelist to establish them for the characters who figure in his story." Sainte-Beuve is the example Wilson gives of this ideal reviewer-critic — though elsewhere ("A Modest Self-Tribute") he has said that he knows very little of Sainte-Beuve's writing and was not directly influenced by him; Poe, that American "literary worker" *tout court*, is the nineteenth-century predecessor more frequently invoked.

The success he has had with this plan of work is a matter of record. When in the early 1950's he took the risk of reprinting in two fat volumes nearly two hundred periodical pieces written between 1922 and 1949, and written each time with the steadfast journalistic purpose of producing something readable and immediately interesting, the result impressively confirmed the rough sense that had been gathering in the minds of readers for a quarter of a century: that for nearly every important development in contemporary literature Edmund Wilson was in some way a spokesman — an arbiter of taste, a supplier of perspective, at the least (to adapt his own phrase for Hemingway) a gauge of intellectual morale. Time and again, reading *Classics and Commercials* (1950) and especially *The Shores of Light* (1952), one would find that judgments formulated under pressure of the weekly deadline had proved to be both just and durable; that they somehow contained that sense of the matter which academic historians of literature, with all the advantages of hindsight, were still groping after. In *The Shores of Light*, for example, one could notice his comments on Pound in 1922 ("at heart . . . an incurable provincial"), on Sherwood Anderson's "queer and disquieting impressiveness" (1923), on the artistic intelligence and originality of Ring Lardner (1924), on E. E. Cummings' lyric integrity (1924, 1927), on the "buried streak of hysteria" in Dos Passos (1929), on John Crowe Ransom's "metaphysical" charm and Allen Tate's "special vein of macabre imagination" (1928), or — in a review of *The Pilgrimage of Henry James* (1925) — on how James's last three novels are "not, as Mr. Brooks asserts, fundamentally unreal and weak" but "perhaps the most vigorous, the most heroically conceived" in all his work.

One could notice, too, the unfailing freshness of his testimony. Despite, inevitably, a certain use of journalistic formulas, Wilson rarely seemed to have repeated himself, in the tiresome manner of the special pleader, the performer with only one string to his fiddle. His stance was rather that of the attentive and open-minded common reader, equipped with nothing more nor less than his own version of that ideal civil intelligence to which every actual phenomenon is in some way significant, deserving to be looked into with an appropriate respect and concern. At the same time it was also clear that in so operating Wilson had never bothered to disguise his prejudices and the play of personal taste and distaste in his reactions. More than once he had been led to assert unfashionable judgments which he was quite unable to carry off in the detail — on the poetry of Edna St. Vincent Millay, for example — and to make a point of persisting in them when they met with general incredulity. But this stubbornness had one virtue: It seemed a further guarantee of that personal engage-

ment with his subjects which might commend his opinions even
to those who found them unsatisfactory. In just this respect it
gave his work an air of greater relevance to the actual conditions
in which literature has its existence — as an affair of *these* writers
and *this* reader, struggling within such and such practical circumstances — than, say, the more methodically conceived practice
of American university critics in the heyday of the "new criticism."

For what Edmund Wilson's writing has always served — and
here again we may think of all he has contributed besides criticism proper — is nothing less than Literature itself, in the broad-
est sense. He believes in literature as a humane activity, an index
to civilization; or, if "belief" seems the wrong sort of word, he
trusts it to the point of choosing to live by it. (We may recall his
celebration, in "The Historical Interpretation of Literature," of
all those before him who truly revered "the priesthood of literature," whatever their special notions.) He takes pride in its suc-
cesses; he is endlessly curious about its tribal customs and the
character, the idiosyncrasies, of its practitioners; out of the same
practical dedication he even concerns himself with the outward
dress and appearance of books, insisting in the latter part of his
career that his own be published in a size and shape that make
holding them and turning their pages a sensible pleasure. And
in so doing he continually bestows upon the whole institution of
literature, and reasserts for it, within the fabric of civilization,
something of that vital efficacy the idea of which we usually think
to associate only with the "great" books but which must survive
at a common level of everyday effort and collaboration if it is
to survive at all. For Wilson has never limited "literature," in
the manner of university reading lists and publishers' anthologies,
to the acknowledged masterpieces. He spreads his net to anything written in such a way, by whatever means, that it conveys
some portion of accurate knowledge or fosters some sort of useful

understanding; in such a way, too, that it helps to maintain the serviceability of ordinary written English to these practical ends. He is genuinely interested in what is being done, and whether it is being done well. He can even grant a virtue of sorts ("a certain purity" that demands "a certain respect") to a best seller like *The Robe*, Dr. Lloyd Douglas' interminable parsonage fable of 1942, when he unexpectedly finds that its author, though in a labored, cliché-ridden way, has done what the best of writers must also do with each new work: "he has imagined the whole thing for himself." But when, infrequently, some truly major occasion presents itself, Wilson can rise to it. A tangible pleasure and exhilaration overtake him when a work of the first rank appears, of almost any kind. He reports it as an occasion for general rejoicing. So he greeted *Lady Chatterley's Lover* in 1929 and so, thirty years later, *Doctor Zhivago*; so, too, after World War II, he celebrated the completion of Malraux's *Psychology of Art*, "one of the really great books of our time."

This generosity of attention deserves the gratitude and praise it has received. Is there anyone among Edmund Wilson's contemporaries who has done so much to keep the general literary establishment critically aware of its own passing history and of its inheritances and opportunities? His great service is to have been (to borrow a phrase) a museum without walls: a museum of idiosyncratic design in some respects but open to all and generally reliable in what it mounts for public view. It may well be that Wilson's long persistence in this service has taken a certain obtuseness and vanity on his part — the same amount needed to support his pretensions as a writer of verse and drama or to permit him, as we have seen, to group *I Thought of Daisy* (and not in 1929 when it was new but twenty-five years later when he reissued it) with the mature masterpieces of Proust and Joyce. Certainly he has had need in some form of that complete self-assurance in opinion and judgment that Alfred Noyes would remember from Princeton in 1914–15, which made Noyes doubt "whether it had ever occurred to him that he could possibly be wrong." (In *A Prelude* Wilson disputes the accuracy of Alfred Noyes's recollections.) The defects of Wilson's singular virtues must be considered. But the essential fact remains: that he has served the collective enterprise of literature in his day with an extraordinary practical energy and faithfulness. By continuing to act as if it really was alive and kicking, he has helped it as much as any critic of his time actually to remain so. His whole career has been a kind of optimistic gamble: he has bet on litera- ture and on its survival — literature as it was in those rich epochs of human history that produced the work his own strong appe- tite as a reader was nurtured on — and he has never seriously hedged this bet.

It may be added that he has carried through this lifelong gamble with a contagious show of willingness and spirit. The way he characterized himself in his "All-Star Literary Vaudeville" of 1926 identifies his outlook still. He is one who has felt "a certain human sympathy" with all manifestations of literary ac- tivity, "even with those of which, artistically, he disapproves." It is a source of deep gratification to him when literature is "sold" to the public, and he is happy to be known as one who "on principle, in the face of alien attack . . . will stand by even the least intelligent, the least disinterested, of its salesmen: he has served in that army himself."

The word Wilson has used for his general attitude is "human- istic." It is not an attitude he has ever troubled to define pre- cisely or to formalize as an objective standard. (But it is not to be confused with the so-called "New Humanism" that was the focus of aggressive controversy in the United States around

1930, a movement of censorious academicians which, because of its arrogant dismissal of nearly everything in literature but the greatest of established classics, Wilson himself attacked with unusual polemic sharpness — see his "Notes on Babbitt and More" of 1930.) Wilson's "humanism" involves first of all an attitude toward the intensity and confusion of ordinary human life. "Poor male and female human beings," he wrote in one of his earliest reviews, of Byron's letters (1922), by way of rejecting the easy moralism that, finding an author like Byron to have been disorderly in his private life and to have brought suffering to others, occupies itself with calling him names — "Poor male and female human beings, who, understanding life in different fashions and unfitted to live together, yet cannot leave each other alone!" (This same outlook is strikingly voiced on the last page of *I Thought of Daisy*.) To be both truthful and sympathetic in one's response to life as it really unfolds, according to the common exactions of human nature, is for Wilson indispensable to a healthy interest in literature, which in turn has value not only as it stays close to concrete experience but as it teaches us this magnanimity of outlook. If, behind particular works of literature seemingly eloquent and well formed, we discover lives and feelings that are sordid, undisciplined, even criminal, we have no reason to turn against these works themselves, or to find fault with the extravagance, perhaps the insincerity, of the imaginative countermeasures they are seen to contain. For art, the Byron piece affirms, "has its origin in the need to pretend that human life is something other than it is, and, in a sense, by pretending this, it succeeds to some extent in transforming it."

This generalized "humanism," as it finds expression in particular critical judgments, is traditional and familiar to a fault. The positivistic Victorian conception of literature as a "criticism of life," basically uplifting in purpose, is still at the core of it; the

sense of what "life" is has simply been brought up to date, to fit
the greater freedom and outspokenness of post-Victorian literary
manners. It is a measure of value which Wilson tends to make
explicit, however, only at odd moments, as when he wishes to
round out an argumentative sequence or give special weight to
some particularly mettlesome opinion. Then we may find it stated
quite baldly, even primly, as if for a moment we were listening
not to a free-minded partisan of modernism in art and thought
but to one of those moralizing schoolmasters whose habit of
literary judgment Edmund Wilson claimed to have shaken off
in his adolescence.

Trying to formulate his distaste for Aldous Huxley's later work,
which he saw as rising out of a rootless detachment from common
human experience, he casually proposed this criterion: the writing we support must help us "to find out something of value for
the control and ennoblement of life" (1941). "It is the part of
an educated man," he remarked in criticizing (as well he might)
the reductive cynicism of the reporting in the magazine *Time*,
"to try to give life some value and point" ("Thoughts on Being
Bibliographed," 1943). Writing with delight and approval of the
"malevolent gusto" of caricature in Angus Wilson's stories, he nevertheless was finally critical of a vision that never showed anything
but "ugliness and humiliation," that seemed to withhold even
pity: "There ought to be some noble value somewhere" (1950).
At times, on this ground, Wilson can bluster like the rankest
Philistine. How little Picasso's art has to offer, he declares, "to-
wards the vindication of human dignity" (1965).

As a memoirist, too, Wilson has regularly spoken the same
language, and spoken it effectively; he falls back on words of old-
fashioned moral approbation with an unembarrassed bluffness
that, following some cogent recital of leading details, can positively
rescue these words from cant and preachiness. A piece on the death

of Elinor Wylie (1929) moves from a straightforward assessment
of his subject's artistic virtues and limitations to praise of her
personal nobility, her grace and perseverance through emotional
dislocations and against the threat of death, and then to a peroration (moving despite its audibly Proustian origin) on what such
a spirit means to the rest of us — "doubtful human creatures,
all quarrelling or herding together, knowing little and thinking
less, vague, pig-headed, purblind and violent" — when we come
upon it in life or in a book. His direct sense of Edna Millay's
gallantry as a person, of some "invincible magnanimity" and "im-
partiality" of mind that distinguished her from the run of asser-
tive talents in her time and that made it impossible not to fall
in love with her, surely underlies his obstinate overvaluation of
her poems. Correspondingly, he several times attacked not
only as inappropriate and misleading but as "unhumanistic"
the formulas of "ironic belittlement" that biography in the Lytton
Strachey manner had made fashionable, though he recognized the
individual brilliance of Strachey's own work. This attitude is
a leitmotif in his major books as well. Perhaps the solidest impression we carry away from *To the Finland Station* is of the
individual moral heroism of the great Marxist leaders and its
ultimate ascendancy in the convulsions of modern history — the
tenacious idealism of Marx himself, surmounting all his human
failures and weaknesses; the disinterested passion of Lenin, the
truly "good-natured man" turned world revolutionary.

There is in fact a good deal of the hero-worshipper in Edmund
Wilson. For a critic whose purpose has been to make what he
admires accessible to others, one must say that there are far
worse things to be. The fine essays on John Jay Chapman, on
"Mr. Rolfe," on Justice Holmes, which are among his most satis-
fying performances, testify to the usefulness to him of this particular moral attitude. Indeed the bulk of Wilson's work in criticism

can plausibly be seen as the record of a quest for a legitimate authority; its root impulse a yearning for the reassurance offered by a certain kind of completed, independent, authoritative image of personality, to which his critical intelligence could honorably attach itself. (Thus his passing allegiance to Marxism seems biographical and literary in inspiration rather than philosophically reasoned.) But for the most part there has been nothing narrow-minded, nothing foolishly restrictive, about the way this impulse has been expressed. Anyone "who works in good faith in his own field," however precious or marginal or even perverse the result may be, anyone who is professionally committed to the thing he does and who goes about it with integrity and, so to speak, professional courage, is likely to win some kind of commendation from him. Early and late, some of Wilson's most characteristic studies are of minor artists and popular entertainers who have caught his attention in this way — Firbank, Max Beerbohm, Genevieve Taggard, Herbert Croly as an editor, the cartoonists Art Young and Sem, Edward Gorey, or the magician Houdini ("an audacious and independent being, whose career showed a rare integrity"). It was in writing about Houdini that Wilson candidly described the radically subjective response that regularly lends feeling and conviction to his exercise of critical judgment: "It is exhilarating, even in a juggler, even in a trapeze performer, to see some human skill or faculty carried to its furthest point, to a point where its feats seem incredible" (1928).

We may say that Wilson's "humanism," whatever its limitations, has finally this virtue: it rests on the knowledge that efforts to derive systems of value from anything but discoverable human experience, or in disregard of any part of discoverable human experience, will fail. The breadth of his tolerance and curiosity as a critic has beneath it this principled concern for admitting the unpleasantest truth about man's life, as does also his special appreciation of works, including diaries and collections of letters, which in any way bring to light the more remarkable conditions of human life and demonstrate its latent further possibilities. So, choking down his revulsion, he labors through the documents in the case of the Marquis de Sade, stopping now and then to note the disingenuousness of attempts to softpedal the real horror of Sade's mind and work, earnestly hoping that his vogue is passing, but granting him the "queer distinction" of having expressed "the ultimate blasphemy" of his (and modern history's) "contempt for human life" with an "ultimate audacity" (1952). It is a point of honor with Wilson, as a critical journalist, to follow to whatever atrocious extreme an accomplished writer may have chosen to lead him.

But every so often Wilson's generosity of attention, his fine critical alertness and receptivity, stop curiously short and are succeeded by obstinate disapproval. An interesting case is his response in the 1940's to Kafka. The chief document here is a *New Yorker* essay of 1947, "A Dissenting Opinion on Kafka." Its journalistic occasion was the appearance of a collected edition of Kafka's writings (which Wilson welcomed as a publishing venture) along with a number of secondary works representing the sudden flaring of a cult-fashion in which as sensible a writer as Delmore Schwartz could suggest that every word Kafka had written was sacred.

Wilson's main objection is to the cult, and to the evidence that Kafka is being "wildly overdone" by demoralized intellectuals who, in their contempt for themselves and for human life in general, are "building him up as a theologian and saint," probably as part of some sinister religious revival. But the full essay, in its zeal to make a case, becomes a gross parody of Wilson's usual humane attentiveness of consideration. Debater's absurdities of in-

nuendo give the argument away. If Kafka is religious, as his de-
votees say, why don't his characters show the "moral fortitude"
of Bunyan's Christian? Where is the "control and direction"
shown by a religious poet like Dante? And how in any case can
Kafka's books be called religious in implication when it is obvious
that he himself "could never let go of the world — of his family,
of his job, of his yearning for bourgeois happiness — in the interest of divine revelation"? There *was* a certain "spiritual charge"
in Kafka, but "you cannot have a first-rate saint or prophet [!]
without a faith of a very much higher potential than is ever to
be felt" in his work.

The coarseness and confusion of argument in this are shock-
ing — and may seem, when they take the form of suggesting that
Kafka's mistake was to make writing "not merely an art but also
somehow a pursuit of righteousness" and "a form of prayer,"
positively dishonest to anyone who remembers Edmund Wilson
as a sympathetic historian of Symbolism, where such doubleness
of purpose was fundamental; in *Axel's Castle* Wilson had noted
reactionary and anti-humanist elements in the writers examined
but had celebrated them all for waking us through their artistic
mastery "to the hope and exaltation of the untried, unsuspected
possibilities of human thought and art." So one hastens to point
out that elsewhere ("A Treatise on Tales of Horror," 1944) Wilson
had already spoken of Kafka as "a master," at least the equal
of Gogol and Poe, whose narratives, at once "satires on the bour-
geoisie and visions of moral horror," are always compellingly logi-
cal and go straight to the imaginative heart of their subjects "with
none of the puppetry of specters and devils" used by run-of-the-
mine fantasists. And in praising George Grosz only a few months
before the Kafka diatribe, Wilson had used the term "Kafka-
esque" — like everybody else in the forties — to sum up Grosz's
vision of Germany on the threshold of Hitlerism.

In 1944 he had been unsure whether Kafka's work and the popular taste for it represented "a retrogression or a progress in the development of modern literature in general," but in 1947 he seems merely priggish, and worse. Kafka — who is somehow to blame for being "denationalized, discouraged, disaffected" as a person: as if a consumptive Czech Jew working as a clerk in a disability claims office during the last decade of the Austro-Hungarian empire was likely to be anything else — "can in the end only let us down. He is quite true to his time and place, but it is surely a time and place in which few of us will want to linger . . ." A cash prize, one thinks, to the reader who can tell that this is not J. Donald Adams but Edmund Wilson. If a critic's "humanism" is finally a matter of not wanting to be "let down" or made to linger in discouraging situations, what virtue is there in it?

What happened in this instance? Leaving aside the provocations of cult-worship (Kafka fanatics *could* be unnerving in 1947), one suspects that Kafka's very artistry, his seamless rendering of an appallingly complete and self-authenticating vision, came too close to certain of Wilson's own fears and cherished fantasies. One point in Wilson's indictment is that unlike Dante, who asserts the classical standard of virtue, "Kafka is at his most characteristic when he is assimilating men to beasts — dogs, insects, mice and apes." But this (which will hardly pass as a description of the moral logic of "Metamorphosis" or even "Investigations of a Dog") is precisely what Wilson himself has regularly done in his satires and polemics, from the moralized dialogue between zoologist and iguana that he wrote in 1925 to the behaviorist swagger of the chapter on sex in *A Piece of My Mind* in 1956 or the wastefully overwritten "Introduction" to *Patriotic Gore* in 1962. There is also the fact that Kafka's work *is* religious in its accomplished grasp: it is religious — rabbinical and Kierkegaardian derivations apart — in the root sense of binding together and sustaining with a rapt simplicity of style a fully apprehended and endured totality of events and impressions which are absolute to experience but remain separately inexplicable. With Kafka as with Biblical narrative, or with a work like *Dr. Zhivago* that Wilson rightly venerates, narrative substantiation of a folklorish definiteness and transparency (including dialogue) is always primary. And what may have been most subtly offensive about Kafka's writings to Edmund Wilson, who has never ceased to boast of the fact that he saw through religion when he was in prep school ("a delusion entertained by other people which one has to try to allow for and understand"), was their undistractible confirmation of the possibility that the religious apprehension of experience is as "real" as the rationalistic, and as absolute an expression of free creative human consciousness. Exposing the doctrinal absurdities advanced in the name of religion (the great game of the fundamentalist freethinkers of Wilson's youth) hardly touches the question of its normative place in human life and history.

The Kafka episode raises with particular sharpness the problem of Wilson's lasting value as a critic and literary worker. There is the question of his working method, and there is the question of the quality of his intelligence, the depth and freedom of mind from which his humanistic judgment proceeds.

As we have seen, Wilson's approach to his subjects is essentially descriptive: he tells the story of careers (his remarks on Kafka are, as usual, chiefly biographical); he summarizes plots, paraphrases arguments, tabulates symbols; he practices psychological description, classification of genres, structural comparison, and various other incidental skills. But he does not analyze, or sufficiently persist in analysis; he does not measure and weigh the constituent ideas; he does not inquire, except biographically, into the whole logic and mode of existence of the works surveyed. In

short, for all his devotion to the idea of literature, he does not
examine and plainly define the specifically literary, architectonic
virtues his arguments assume. His interest regularly turns off
to the special matter of the psychology of literary behavior, to
what he speaks of in "The Historical Interpretation of Literature"
as "the attitudes, the compulsions, the emotional 'patterns' that
recur in the work of a writer." What was it like, in terms of
familiar human emotions, to have been this or that author at
the moment of composing such and such a work? — a legitimate
question but incidental to the primary and distinguishing concerns of literary criticism. (In *Axel's Castle*, for example, we
find this rare formulation of critical theory: "The real elements,
of course, of any work of fiction, are the elements of the author's
personality." It is a notion, one must say, which crops up strangely
in a chapter, on Proust, that has been largely occupied with com-
menting on a controlled artistic structure of an extraordinary
compositional complexity, and in a book that has set out to demonstrate the existence of a broad historical "movement" characterized by various "common tendencies.") On this ground, view-
ing literature as a species of personal expression, Wilson takes
what appears before him, what is given, and describes it according
to his lights. But he is without the disciplined interest in what
could be or might be or even should be that makes the great critic,
the writer on literature who will alter the very foundations of
critical judgment and who may even project (as, in earlier American criticism, Poe did) new images of creative personality for literary history to advance by.

There is point to such reservations — certainly we have to
distinguish between the service of an Edmund Wilson to critical
understanding in his time and the service of a Poe, a James, an
Eliot — but first the virtues of his manner may be considered.
Who his closest practical models have been is not difficult to

discover. He has been explicit about them, and insofar as they have also served as models for his justly admired prose style, with its clarity, efficiency, and steady forwarding energy, we cannot say offhand that they have been bad models. One of the most important was his teacher at Princeton, Christian Gauss; and in Wilson's memorial account of the method of Gauss's teaching we find a clear statement of his own chosen procedure as a critic. The special quality in Gauss, Wilson writes, was "the unusual fluidity of mind that he preserved through his whole career." As against a dogmatist like Irving Babbitt, Gauss was the kind of teacher "who starts trains of thought that he does not himself guide to conclusions but leaves in the hands of his students to be carried on by themselves." Moreover, "his own ideas on any subject were always taking new turns: the light in which he saw it would be shifted, it would range itself in some new context." Gauss knew a great deal about a great many things, and had the knowledge of languages to back up his literary and historical learning. But he carried this learning unostentatiously. His easy manner, his level voice, Wilson says (apparently without irony), "made a kind of neutral medium in which everything in the world seemed soluble."

The result was an impression of "extreme flexibility and enormous range"—of a mind whose powers could be brought to bear with equal force on any important subject—and in describing Gauss's method Wilson is clearly projecting a view of his own. Gauss, he writes, was "able to explain and appreciate almost any kind of work of literature from almost any period. He would show you what the author was aiming at and the methods he had adopted to achieve his ends." And he had "a knack of fixing in one's mind key passages and key facts." At the same time he was distinctly at his best in presenting an established figure whose relative stature and significance might be open to more questions

31

than he cared to deal with but whose claim to attention was beyond dispute. Rousseau is the example Wilson cites, and in his account of how Gauss would highlight the main incidents in Rousseau's career—a writer whom students were likely to find boring—"by a series of incisive strokes that [nevertheless] involved no embroidery or dramatics," we see what the technique was. Gauss would bring a Rousseau forward to the turning point; the moment when, going to visit Diderot in prison, he decided to compete for the essay prize on the question of whether progress in the arts and sciences had tended to corrupt or to purify society; the moment when he set out for the "Finland station" of his life's progress. Gauss also set a standard for style that Wilson respected and mastered. "He made us all want to write something in which every word, every cadence, every detail, should perform a definite function in producing an intense effect."

Another of Wilson's models of critical procedure (leaving aside models of style and intellectual temper like Shaw, Samuel Butler, Renan, H. L. Mencken) was Saintsbury, and again, professing admiration for Saintsbury's *Encyclopaedia Britannica* articles, he gives us a passage of self-definition, praising those "wonderful feats of condensation that manage, in summarizing a lifetime, to include a maximum of detail and, in their briefly expressed comments, to hit all the nails on the head." Saintsbury was "perhaps the only English critic, with the possible exception of Leslie Stephen, whose work is comparable, for comprehensiveness and brilliance, to the great French critics [Taine in particular] of the nineteenth century." But Wilson also remarks that unlike these latter, Saintsbury "has no interest in ideas"—and we recall our reservations about Wilson's own performance. He himself clearly has had an *interest* in ideas, but it has been an oddly acquiescent and derivative interest. He observes them, like natural phenomena; he wonders what drives men to take them up, and he is impressed by the power that derives from them; but he does not seem to *think* with them, or about them, or make them — at least provisionally — his own. He does not seem to have imagined what exactly it means to say that thought, in our own case as well as for those history presents, must be proved in experience.

Wilson has always seemed admirably free of ideological dogmatism and pre-commitment and especially alert to how other minds and lives may be warped by them — one reason why he has been so effective as a natural historian of the literary life. But there is something static about this liberal curiosity of his, something curiously automatic and self-enclosed. What Santayana said once about American open-mindedness in general applies to it: that it can too easily turn into "a habit of doting on everything" — everything, that is, that happens to have caught its attention; that it derives from a personal assurance it never stops to test, which is that "the forces that determine fortune are not yet too complicated for one man to explore"; that it trusts its own accumulated habituations as it trusts nothing else, because it has always been able to do so "safely and prosperously." If we read a lot of Edmund Wilson's criticism at one time, what we may come to notice is less and less the free play of this curiosity and the insights and discoveries it leads him to, and more and more the a priori assurance it rests upon — and in this regard the mind which most resembles his own or which his own most resembles is that of his father, the Red Bank, New Jersey, lawyer to whom he devoted the last section of his book of "reflections at sixty," *A Piece of My Mind.*

For it is very much a *type* of mind that Wilson's writing gives voice to, a distinctly American type perhaps, at least a familiar and important one in both American literature and American

WARNER BERTHOFF

public life. An otherwise excellent study of his career written some years ago by Norman Podhoretz labeled him "the last patrician," which is of course inaccurate; whoever our American patricians may be, they have had little to do with our serious literature. His mold is rather his father's — the mold of the independent, freethinking professional man, in this case of the type of the town or small-city lawyer (a newspaper editor or certain types of businessman would do about as well; a doctor, teacher, minister less well); the man of broad but not particularly fine taste, with a strong and confident habit of mind and with pride in his judgment, who is skillful at dossiers, presentations of essential evidence, summings-up; something of a dissenter but according to no easily predictable pattern, and certainly not one of shallow self-interest; conservatively radical, out of an unshakable assurance about his own privileged position; a leader of opinion used to making himself listened to (but not likely to be aware that among those who have come to know him well, as opposed to the public at large, a silent resistance is steadily building up); a champion of seemingly unpopular causes, but not so much lost causes as certain ones not yet effectively taken up; one whom we visualize finally rather as Edmund Wilson portrays his father, "explaining at length, but with an expert lucidity, some basic point of law or government."

This breed of mind, which seems raised to a virtuoso perfection in the two Edmund Wilsons, has substantial virtues. It is intelligent and accurate. It can be trained into great practical skill. It will give steady, efficient, profitable performance. It admires things worth admiring; it has a sense of "excellence" (a favorite word); it is alert to prevailing tendencies. It understands Darwinism and Freudianism — it used to understand Marxism — and modern anthropology and, nowadays, the theory of the genetic code and the notion of complementarity and perhaps

34

the eightfold way. It is at ease with literary and philosophical classics and is given to more or less appropriate citations from them in support of its point of view. It only lacks the ability to see beyond itself. And it is not so much without the power to do this as without the inward incentive, the imaginative will. For it is finally an arrogant and airless mind. It is acquainted with a great many ideas, but ideas become things to it, counters to score with. Its besetting sin is in fact *knowingness*, which is its substitute for imaginative freedom and the passion of irreversible creative conviction. And whatever else knowingness is good for, it cannot cure itself; it cannot intercede against those particular afflictions, "complacency and resentment," which Camus in a late essay identified as peculiar to the writer's, the intellectual's, course of life.

Far more than any particular miscarriage of critical judgment, it is this element of knowingness that disturbs us in Edmund Wilson's writing. We come to sense a kind of incapacity to imagine that what he knows or has found out is not always the whole essential story, and that what others see, which he himself cannot see, may nevertheless really be there. We see finally that his curiosity and liberality are of a special kind. Like his father, Wilson accepts the system he works within, in this case the literary establishment and its received custom — about which he makes it his business to keep very well informed. He does not fundamentally question this system. He only aspires to master it (which he is willing to work hard to do) and then to have his mastery acknowledged. When something comes into view that does not fit the measure of this system or that would expose the accommodations it is built on to some ulterior judgment — the Kafka case is one instance; Eliot's writing, with its inner burden of religious nostalgia and reversion, is another — liberal curiosity may give way abruptly to irritation and withdrawal.

Irritability, resentment, the impatient dismissal of what cannot be absorbed without a basic recasting of his own fixed attitudes, appear to be Edmund Wilson's characteristic vices; and the point to be made about them is that they are not merely personal failings but the intellectual expedients of a whole identifiable class. His postures as a critic are those of the privileged and established old resident, American style — we picture him on a balcony or at an upstairs window overlooking the town, a county seat perhaps (for he is a man of the world) — beset by uneasiness at some of the changes taking place before him but not compelled to add them all up and arrive at a genuinely new sum. The system he contemplates he imagines to be for him and he does not mean to see it fundamentally changed, but in his own mind he stands outside it. There he perches, coolly examining the credentials of oldtimers and newcomers alike as they pass in review; examining them shrewdly and fairly, to be sure, but nevertheless with the limited purposes of a chronicler of settlement. He is interested in much that is irregular and judged by others to be unworthy of a reputable mind's concern: burlesque shows, popular cartoonists, sentimental best sellers, the Marquis de Sade. But he tends to give his full attention and approval only to those who lend themselves to his developed methods of treatment, who provide him with a trustworthy professional occasion.

Here again Wilson's portrait of his lawyer-father mirrors his own professional character and identifies something central to his whole effort as a critic. "The reason for his success [in the practice of law] was undoubtedly that he never undertook a case which he did not think he could win, and that his judgment about this was infallible. In court, he attacked the jury with a mixture of learning, logic, dramatic imagination and eloquence which he knew would prove irresistible. He would cause them to live through the events of the crime or supposed crime, he would take them through the steps of the transaction, whatever this was, and he would lodge in their heads a picture that it was difficult for his opponent to expel." Such a man is hard to argue with. One can only point to what has been left out, provided one has sufficient knowledge of the case oneself and has not been charmed into overlooking the omissions.

And in all of Wilson's writing, most strikingly in his three major works of sustained exposition — *Axel's Castle, To the Finland Station, Patriotic Gore* — there are, given the designated subject, notable omissions. We must be fair to Wilson on this point and grant that the format of these books — each is presented as a "study" or set of "studies" and not as a definitive history — allows him a broad margin for choice and special emphasis within the scope of the subject as a whole. As it happens, however, the pattern of emphasis and omission significantly affects the historical case each book develops. The broad criticism climaxing *Axel's Castle*, that the Symbolist tradition encourages an ivory-tower withdrawal from the objective world and in particular from society, is made easier to sustain by the fact that the field has been limited to French- and English-speaking examples (easier, also, through the inclusion of Gertrude Stein, who is in no proper sense a Symbolist). The story would be interestingly different if important Russian and German Symbolists had been introduced — Blok, George, even Rilke, who once eloquently defined his work as proceeding "from the conviction that it is possible to give a pure demonstration of the width, variety, and even the fullness of the world." (Wilson's unfamiliarity with German literature is perhaps the chief defect in his ambitious scheme to be an agent of "general cross-fertilization"; he himself has noted, as his "own worst disqualification," his lack of Spanish and Portuguese, but his disregard of the leading German writers of the modern era has left the more serious gap in the kind of "synoptic" record he has spoken of wanting to establish.)

More important, for *Axel's Castle*, is his disregard of one of the key developments in the ideology of classical French Symbolism: its extreme and uncompromising case against literature itself as a justifiable activity. Surely it was this, and not, as Wilson argues, "a personal crisis" precipitated by "an unhappy love affair," that silenced Valéry as a poet for twenty years. The real choice posed by the pairing off of Axel and Rimbaud in the last chapter is not between the ivory tower and common life but between literature and silence — and in concentrating on the sensational facts of Rimbaud's personal behavior rather than on the critical matter of his furious rejection of the time-serving life of letters in any form, including the visionary, Wilson managed to avoid the profound challenge thrown out by the very tradition he was examining against the whole system of literature he had made it his vocation to serve.

Even within the individual chapters of *Axel's Castle*, one's initial admiration for the fullness and panoramic clarity with which, say, the immense structure of Proust's masterpiece is described and put in order may be modified by second thoughts. Being invited to consider a writer like Proust "in a large context of ideas and history, after so many purely exegetical commentaries," is indeed novel and exhilarating, as Richard Chase remarked on re-reading the book in the late 1950's. But one is also more likely upon a rereading to notice, for example, the absence of any reference whatsoever to the painter Elstir and to the great speculative disquisitions on his art and his progress as an artist. It is like reading an account of the design of *Doctor Zhivago* that failed to mention that novel's moving, simple, and absolutely crucial evocation of the creative process, in its climactic fourteenth chapter.

38

Again, with *To the Finland Station*, the concentrated studies, which are the core of the book's argument, of Marx, Engels, and Lenin as individual agents are vividly persuasive and add a dimension to our knowledge of this great chapter in modern history that we may not have gotten so well from ordinary historians. But the scheme Wilson worked out for the book as a whole calls for an opening section on the decline of the bourgeois revolutionary tradition — against this decline and "disintegration" the emergence of revolutionary socialism in the extreme Marxist-Leninist mold appears both the more heroic and the more inevitable — and here we feel that the scheme derives not from an objective grasp of these momentous developments in modern history but from the accidents of the author's earlier reading; for the figures chosen to represent bourgeois revolutionary decadence are, surprisingly, Renan, Taine, and Anatole France, men of letters all and, as it happens, key figures (they have remained critical touchstones all his life) in the study of French literature he carried out under Christian Gauss at Princeton.

With *Patriotic Gore*, built up more obviously piecemeal during ten years of book-reviewing, the pattern of emphasis and omission can better afford to be irregular and somewhat arbitrary. Yet in a work that presents itself as dealing with the *literature* of the Civil War and that includes a bold hypothesis about the effects of the war on American style and diction, the absence of anything but the most cursory references to Whitman and Melville — each of whom created an imaginative record of the progress of the war that is without parallel in modern literature — is remarkable, to say the least. They are mentioned, and warily praised (*Drum-Taps*, Wilson writes, "certainly contained the best poetry that was written during the war on the subject of the war"), but the possibility that their extraordinary creative originality might provide a deeper insight into the whole experience of the war and contribute a more profoundly truthful response to the book's record of the war's progressive impact is passed over. One begins to appreciate the point of an English reviewer's waspish remark, in another context in the early 1950's, that "Mr. Wilson, as a commentator, seems in his heart to prefer small perishable books to large enduring ones."

It is disappointing, too, considering the detailed attention given to Frederick Goddard Tuckerman and Sidney Lanier, that Emily Dickinson is passed over in half a page. Perhaps this is stretching the point: though the bulk of her finest poetry was in fact written during the first years of the war crisis, the great productive interval in her life, Wilson is correct in saying that she does not allude directly to the war, and we have also to remember his principle of not writing at length on authors who have already been widely discussed, or "overdone." Yet a critic of Wilson's determined sensitivity to the way historical forces impinge on individual imaginations might reasonably be expected to make something out of Emily Dickinson's special eloquence through this period (when New England, its conscience roused, poured out its regiments of volunteers), with her themes of parting, spiritual division, the transforming shock of death, and with her imagery, direct and oblique, of souls at Armageddon. It would be something critically "new," and it would throw a clarifying light on the other testimonies *Patriotic Gore* presents.

Scanting the three great poets of the era (who alone among American authors could fully articulate the same tragic and purgatorial sense of the terrible experience of their time that is expressed in Lincoln's second inaugural) simplifies Wilson's task in psychologizing the conduct and the consequences of the war, North and South. It makes easier the job of imposing a general view of war (given directly in the "Introduction" and strongly insinuated in the stress laid on Calvin Stowe's apocalyptic fantasies or Sherman's manic ruthlessness) as a wholly irrational embodiment of unconscious power drives yielding best to essentially zoological behavior analysis. Clarity and firmness of opinion seem here to have been purchased at too dear a cost. One does not have to be a secret war-lover, or any less opposed to the self-righteousness and hypocrisy that always seek to justify aggressive violence, to feel that Wilson has prejudged the case and that criticism has given way to distemper and invective. Or is it that a desire to separate himself from what to reasoned calculation will always be most disturbing in any great convulsion of human experience, being most problematical and obscure, seems stronger than the wish to know all that may be known? — a desire above all to guard himself against the possibility that for those fully caught up in life, even for the wisest, there may always be something they must do that cannot be properly prepared for or explained, and, moreover, that such moral disorder may be normative for man and not the result of somebody else's having panicked. Some fundamental deficiency in his address to human experience, some incapacity to carry on where the way is not wholly clear, severely inhibits the thrust of Wilson's critical inquiry just as it approaches deep waters. That queer pleasure he has always taken in listing the superficial resemblances of men to animals and insects begins, in its indiscriminate repetitiveness, to appear less and less the expression of a ruthless iconoclasm or moral honesty and more and more a whistling in the dark to keep his courage up.

But once again we find that Wilson himself has given the plainest account of his own case. In *A Prelude*, looking back over his whole life, he writes: "The most painful moments of my life have been due to indecision. I usually know exactly what I want to do, and it has been only when I could not make up my mind that I have really gone to pieces." (What is strangest about wartime conditions in his early story, "The Death of a Soldier," is learn-

41

WARNER BERTHOFF

ing "the habit of not making plans and surrendering the direction of his life"; this becomes in fact the first step in the young soldier's progress toward death.) Correspondingly, in the essay "The Historical Interpretation of Literature," Wilson's final stress is on the "relief" that great works of literature bring us — relief from the element of change and disruptive novelty in our experience, and from the confrontation with those emergent conditions of life which nobody has yet mastered: "With each such victory of the human intellect, whether in history, in philosophy or in poetry, we experience a deep satisfaction; we have been cured of some ache of disorder, relieved of some oppressive burden of uncomprehended events." A negative satisfaction, one is bound to say. Surely the best part of our response to the literature that seems important to us is to the sustained act of original creation it comprises, its surprising augmentation of the life and fortune we must endure in any case, and not merely to some soothing feat of homeopathic exorcism.

Yet we must grant that this appropriation of literature for purposes of creaturely self-defense is related to what has always been most interesting and rewarding in Edmund Wilson's work, and that is his exceptional shrewdness in catching the distinctive character and use of the document before him and in establishing for it (to use his own phrase) a definite literary identity. For the kind of serious journalistic accounting that his work regularly proposes, this is the indispensable virtue. Wilson is consistently quick and definite as a judge of the special quality of individual men. More exactly, he is a good judge of the *testimony* of individual men. (In this respect, too, he is his father's son.) He is a good judge, that is, of men according to their manner of expression in words. In *Patriotic Gore* what he writes about Grant and Sherman on the basis of their written memoirs is perceptive and just. But the kind of panoramic historical criticism he seems

42

to be attempting in this as in his other major books has to be something more than cross-examination and the description of documents — and we notice that what Wilson says of these same men by inference from their conduct in the field and from the general evidence of their behavior in life or of their children's behavior (see the ten pages on Tom Sherman's tormented life) is very much less satisfactory. When it is not the cliché of common gossip and memory, of hero-worship or collective slander, it is mostly behaviorist fantasy. Wilson has a sharp ear for the points at which a man's casual language may have revealed or betrayed him, and he can usually be trusted in descriptions of where and in what ways a writer has put some part of himself into his books. But this is not the same thing as understanding the full historical life such books and documents have emerged from and ambiguously refer to, in which respect Wilson's effort of judgment tends regularly to lapse into a kind of sophisticated sloganeering or name-calling. Again, we feel the lack of any controlling idea that is appropriate, and sufficient, to the full dimensions of the subject.

We see, in short, that Edmund Wilson's critical intelligence operates most persuasively on the words people leave behind them, but that as his inquiry draws him on into speculation about the reasons for these words and the human motives, actions, necessities they incorporate, this verbal positivism — the very quality that gives his literary chronicling its admirable particularity and common sense — becomes more obstruction than asset. We notice in *To the Finland Station* and *Patriotic Gore* that his comparisons and definitions are nearly always in terms of other books, and that he is most effective in comparing minor and uncomplicated matters to familiar situations in guaranteed classics: thus the South Carolina Chesnuts are like the Bolkonskys in *War and Peace*, an episode in their life is like Chekhov, and

43

so on. (So he himself wrote in 1922 of the insulated bookishness of Ezra Pound: "everything in life only serves to remind him of something in literature.") When such comparisons do not turn up, he seems at a loss to know what to think. And the suspicion rises again that perhaps this praiseworthy belief in the efficacy and validity of literature-as-such is damagingly related, in Edmund Wilson's case, to some profound distrust of life and all its disconcerting profusion of motives and appearances; a constitutional distrust of the mind's freedom to act, its power to keep balance, against such profusion; a chronic personal insecurity that issues in these strained countermeasures of hero-worship and aggressive irritability. It may be sound tactics for a journalist on roving commission to work from such motives. It can be a guarantee of directness and authenticity of relation. But it is a handicap, one must say, in the serious prosecution of a sustained historical argument.

But that being said, the fact remains that Edmund Wilson's service as a writer on literature and contemporary events has been for nearly half a century a singularly valuable and important one. Again and again, returning to his essays, we are reminded how much we depend on first-rate critical journalism of the kind he has provided and how rare a thing it is, how poor we are without it. Even more than readers, writers need it — need from their apprenticeship a reliable court of appeals, sympathetic yet discriminating, tireless in its devotion to special cases, liberally informed, indifferent to ideological clamor and extraneous systems of valuation; a court that can be trusted to respond to their work directly and on its own presented terms but that can also remember its developing character from one effort to the next and so help gain for each author treated the status, the clarifying dignity and coherence, of a recognizable career.

That is to say, literature itself — whatever further history lies in store for it — needs such writing. And it is hard to imagine American literature in all the decades since 1920 without the assisting presence of Edmund Wilson. For several successive literary generations he has continued as a critical observer to make the whole enterprise of literature seem an enterprise immensely worth participating in and extending further. It has been a worthy service, richly deserving the honor and respect it has brought him. And nothing, now, seems more agreeably in character than Wilson's businesslike way of playing his part as a literary elder statesman. Refusing to retire into a merely ceremonial eminence, he continues to observe and to offer his affirmative comment: a still reliable measure of present value, a practical source of encouragement for any future we can bear to imagine.

⚹ Selected Bibliography

Principal Works of Edmund Wilson

The Undertaker's Garland (with John Peale Bishop). New York: Knopf, 1922.

Discordant Encounters: Plays and Dialogues. New York: Boni, 1926.

I Thought of Daisy. New York: Scribner's, 1929.

Poets, Farewell! New York: Scribner's, 1929.

Axel's Castle: A Study in the Imaginative Literature of 1870 to 1930. New York and London: Scribner's, 1931.

The American Jitters: A Year of the Slump. New York and London: Scribner's, 1932.

Travels in Two Democracies. New York: Harcourt, Brace, 1936.

This Room and This Gin and These Sandwiches: Three Plays. New York: New Republic, 1937.

The Triple Thinkers: Ten Essays on Literature. New York: Harcourt, Brace, 1938.

To the Finland Station: A Study in the Writing and Acting of History. New York: Harcourt, Brace, 1940.

The Boys in the Back Room: Notes on California Novelists. San Francisco: Colt Press, 1941.

The Wound and the Bow: Seven Studies in Literature. Boston: Houghton Mifflin, 1941.

Note-Books of Night. San Francisco: Colt Press, 1942.

The Shock of Recognition: The Development of Literature in the United States Recorded by the Men Who Made It (anthology). Garden City, N.Y.: Doubleday, Doran, 1943.

Memoirs of Hecate County. Garden City, N.Y.: Doubleday, 1946.

Europe without Baedeker: Sketches among the Ruins of Italy, Greece, and England. Garden City, N.Y.: Doubleday, 1947.

Classics and Commercials: A Literary Chronicle of the Forties. New York: Farrar, Straus, 1950.

The Shores of Light: A Literary Chronicle of the Twenties and Thirties. New York: Farrar, Straus and Young, 1952.

Eight Essays. Garden City, N.Y.: Anchor Books (Doubleday), 1954.

Five Plays. New York: Farrar, Straus and Young, 1954.

The Scrolls from the Dead Sea. New York: Oxford University Press, 1955.

Red, Black, Blond and Olive: Studies in Four Civilizations: Zuñi, Haiti, Soviet Russia, Israel. New York: Oxford University Press, 1956.

A Piece of My Mind: Reflections at Sixty. New York: Farrar, Straus and Cudahy, 1956.

The American Earthquake: A Documentary of the Twenties and Thirties. New York: Doubleday, 1958.

Apologies to the Iroquois. New York: Farrar, Straus and Cudahy, 1960.

Night Thoughts. New York: Farrar, Straus and Cudahy, 1961.

Patriotic Gore: Studies in the Literature of the American Civil War. New York: Oxford University Press, 1962.

The Cold War and the Income Tax. New York: Farrar, Straus, 1963.

O Canada: An American's Notes on Canadian Culture. New York: Farrar, Straus and Giroux, 1965.

The Bit between My Teeth: A Literary Chronicle of 1950–1965. New York: Farrar, Straus and Giroux, 1965.

A Prelude: Landscapes, Characters and Conversations from the Earlier Years of My Life. New York: Farrar, Straus and Giroux, 1967.

Biographical and Critical Studies

Aaron, Daniel. *Writers on the Left.* New York: Harcourt, Brace and World, 1961.

Brown, E. K. "The Method of Edmund Wilson," *University of Toronto Quarterly*, 11:105–11 (October 1941).

"A Critic and His Time," *Times Literary Supplement*, 2877:240 (April 19, 1957).

Hicks, Granville. "The Intransigence of Edmund Wilson," *Antioch Review*, 6:550–62 (Winter 1946–47).

Howe, Irving. "Edmund Wilson: A Revaluation," *Nation*, 167:430–33 (October 16, 1948).

Hyman, Stanley Edgar. "Edmund Wilson and Translation in Criticism," *The Armed Vision.* New York: Knopf, 1948.

"The Influence of Edmund Wilson," *Nation*, 186:159–70 (February 22, 1958). (Essays by Robert E. Spiller, Richard Chase, Robert Cantwell.)

Kaufmann, R. J. "The Critic as Custodian of Sanity," *Critical Quarterly*, 1:85–98 (Summer 1959).

Paul, Sherman. *Edmund Wilson: A Study of Literary Vocation in Our Time.* Urbana: University of Illinois, 1965.

Perényi, Eleanor. "Wilson," *Esquire*, 60:80–85, 188 (July 1963).

Podhoretz, Norman. "Edmund Wilson: Then and Now," *Doings and Undoings.* New York: Farrar, Straus and Giroux, 1964.

Schwartz, Delmore. "The Writing of Edmund Wilson," *Accent*, 2:177–86 (Spring 1942).

Wain, John. "Edmund Wilson," *Essays on Literature and Ideas.* London: Macmillan, 1963.

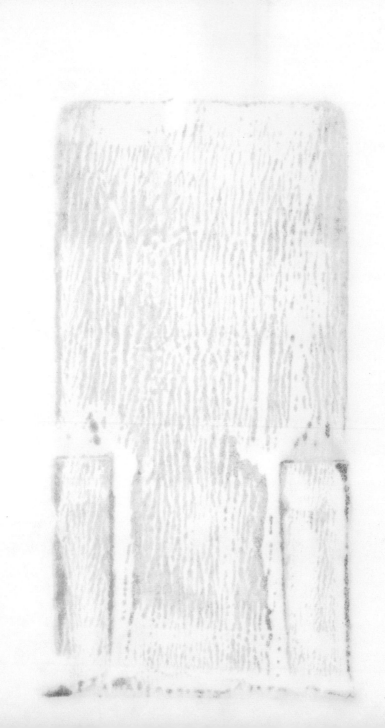

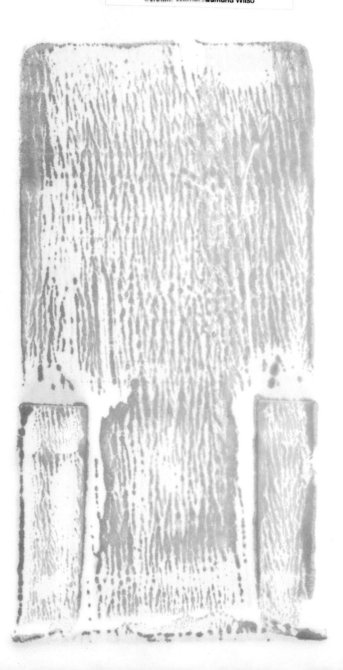